God is Love

The C. R. Gibson Company
Norwalk, Connecticut

*He that loveth not
knoweth not God;
for God is love.*

I JOHN 4:8

The heart of him who truly loves is a paradise on
earth; he has God in himself, for God is love.
FÉLICITÉ ROBERT de LAMENNAIS

There's a wideness in God's mercy
Like the wideness of the sea,
There is kindness in His justice
Which is more than liberty.

For the love of God is broader
Than the measure of man's mind,
And the heart of the Eternal
Is most wonderfully kind.
FREDERICK W. FABER

And thou shalt love the Lord thy God with all thy
heart, and with all thy soul, and with all thy mind,
and with all thy strength: this is the first
commandment.
And the second is like, namely this, Thou shalt love
thy neighbour as thyself. There is none other
commandment greater than this.
MARK 12:30,31

Immortal Love, for ever full,
For ever flowing free,
For ever shared, for ever whole,
A never ebbing sea!

Our outward lips confess the Name
All other names above;
Love only knoweth whence it came,
And comprehendeth love.

JOHN GREENLEAF WHITTIER

. . . If God be for us, who can be against us?
ROMANS 8:31

In all the crowded universe
There is but one stupendous word:
Love.
There is no tree that rears its crest,
No fern or flower that cleaves the sod
Nor bird that sings above its nest,
But tries to speak this word of God.
JOSIAH GILBERT HOLLAND

You asked me why we should love God and how much we should love him. I reply that we should love God because He is God and that the measure of our love should be to love Him without measure.

ST. BERNARD OF CLAIRVAUX

For thy dear saints, O Lord,
Who strove in thee to live,
Who followed thee, obeyed, adored,
Our grateful hymn receive.

RICHARD MANT

Beloved, if God so loved us, we ought also to love one another.
No man hath seen God at any time. If we love one another, God dwelleth in us, and his love is perfected in us.
Hereby know we that we dwell in him, and he in us, because he hath given us of his Spirit.

I JOHN 4:11-13

I asked the New Year for some message sweet,
Some rule of life with which to guide my feet;
I asked, and paused: he answered soft and low,
   "God's will to know."

"Will knowledge then suffice, New Year?"
I cried;
And, ere the question into silence died,
The answer came, "Nay, but remember, too,
   God's will to do."

Once more I asked, "Is there no more to tell?"
And once again the answer sweetly fell,
"Yes! this thing, all other things above:
   God's will to love."

ANONYMOUS

As the love of God is man's highest happiness and
blessedness, and the ultimate end and aim of all
human activities, it follows that he alone lives by the
Divine Law who loves God, not from fear of
punishment, or from love of any other object . . . but
solely because he has knowledge of God.
BARUCH SPINOZA

Give free and bold play to those instincts of the heart which believe that the Creator must care for the creatures He has made, and that the only real effective care for them must be that which takes each of them into His love, and knowing it separately surrounds it with His separate sympathy. There is not one life which the Life-giver ever loses out of His sight; not one which sins so that He casts it away; not one which is not so near to Him that whatever touches it touches Him with sorrow or with joy.

PHILLIPS BROOKS

In heavenly love abiding,
        No change my heart shall fear;
And safe is such confiding,
        For nothing changes here.

A. L. WARING

God not only loves us more and better than we can ever love ourselves—but God loved us before we loved, or could love, Him. God's love rendered possible and actual our love of God.

FRIEDRICH von HÜGEL

My Father's world—and yet
For me He leaves stirring, mighty tasks;
And bids me share with Him
In building love and truth and joy
To make His dream come true.

My Father's world—and yet
On me waits part of all the beauty, love,
And tenderness the world
Might use in building other powers
To make His dream come true.

My Father's world—and yet
Not His until each willing child of His,
For Him and for His dream,
Gives love and toil and sacrifice
To make His dream come true.

ANONYMOUS

All His glory and beauty and love come from within,
and there He delights to dwell, His visits there are
frequent, His conversation sweet, His comforts
refreshing; and His peace passeth all understanding.
THOMAS À. KEMPIS

O God,
Thyself the perfection of beauty,
Who lovest all things beautiful
And through them are constantly
Making Thyself known unto man:

Teach us
By the beauty that is in the world
That nothing unbeautiful can live before Thee;

And help our lives
So to clothe themselves in beauty
That even through us
Thy glory may be made manifest.
ANONYMOUS

No one has the capacity to judge God. We are drops in
that limitless ocean of mercy and infinite love.
SENECA

The best way to know God
is to love many things.
VINCENT van GOGH

TO SEE GOD'S LOVE

What inexpressible joy for me, to look
up through the apple-blossoms and the
fluttering leaves, and to see God's love
there; to listen to the thrush that has
built his nest among them, and to feel
God's love, who cares for the birds, in
every note that swells his little throat; to
look beyond to the bright blue depths of
the sky, and to feel they are a canopy of
blessing,—the roof of the house of my
Father; that if the clouds pass over it, it
is the unchangeable light they veil; that,
even when the day itself passes, I shall
see that the night itself only unveils new
worlds of light; and to know that if I
could unwrap fold after fold of God's
universe, I should only unfold more and
more blessing, and see deeper and deeper
into the love which is at the heart of all.
ELIZABETH CHARLES

Our Father, as we start the day,
We think of children far away
In other lands across the sea.
Help us their loving friends to be.
Help all Thy children everywhere
To share Thee and Thy loving care.

AGNES SMYTH KELSEY

Little things, come daily, hourly, within our reach, and
they are not less calculated to set forward our growth
in holiness, than are the greater occasions which occur
but rarely. Moreover, fidelity in trifles, and an earnest
seeking to please God in little matters, is a test of real
devotion and love. Let your aim be to please our dear
Lord perfectly in little things, and to attain a spirit of
childlike simplicity and dependence. In proportion as
self-love and self-confidence are weakened, and our
will bowed to that of God, so will hindrances
disappear, the internal troubles and contests which
harassed the soul vanish, and it will be filled with
peace and tranquillity.

JEAN NICOLAS GROU

OUR DAILY GIFTS

Gratitude consists in a watchful, minute
attention to the particulars of our state,
and to the multitude of God's gifts,
taken one by one. It fills us with a
consciousness that God loves and cares
for us, even to the least event and the
smallest need of life. It is a blessed
thought, that from our childhood God
has been laying His fatherly hands upon
us, and always in benediction; that even
the strokes of His hands are blessings,
and among the chiefest we have ever
received. When this feeling is awakened,
the heart beats with a pulse of
thankfulness. Every gift has its return of
praise. It awakens an unceasing daily
converse with our Father,—He speaking
to us by the descent of blessings, we to
Him by the ascent of thanksgiving. And
all our whole life is thereby drawn under
the light of His countenance, and is
filled with a gladness, serenity, and peace
which only thankful hearts can know.
HENRY EDWARD MANNING

Though I speak with the tongues of men and of angels, and have not charity, I am become as sounding brass, or a tinkling cymbal.
And though I have the gift of prophecy, and understand all mysteries, and all knowledge; and though I have all faith, so that I could remove mountains, and have not charity, I am nothing.
And though I bestow all my goods to feed the poor, and though I give my body to be burned, and have not charity, it profiteth me nothing.
Charity suffereth long, and is kind; charity envieth not; charity vaunteth not itself, is not puffed up, Beareth all things, believeth all things, hopeth all things, endureth all things. Charity never faileth . . .

I CORINTHIANS 13:1-4;7,8

On Thy compassion I repose
    In weakness and distress:
I will not ask for greater ease,
    Lest I should love Thee less;
Oh, 'tis a blessed thing for me
    To need Thy tenderness.

A. L. WARING

I find the most convincing evidence of Him . . . in the quiet testimony of beauty, truth, love, goodness, peace, joy, self-sacrifice, and a consecration, which point to another kind of world within the one we see and touch.

RUFUS JONES

Be Thou my Sun, my selfishness destroy,
Thy atmosphere of Love be all my joy;
Thy Presence be my sunshine ever bright,
My soul the little mote that lives but in Thy light.

GERHARD TERSTEEGEN

Oh, look not at thy pain or sorrow, how great soever; but look from them, look off them, look beyond them, to the Deliverer! whose power is over them, and whose loving, wise, and tender Spirit is able to do thee good by them. The Lord lead thee, day by day, in the right way, and keep thy mind stayed upon Him, in whatever befalls thee; that the belief of His love and hope in His mercy, when thou art at the lowest ebb, may keep up thy head above the billows.

ISAAC PENINGTON

HOUSEHOLD PRAYER

Lord of all pots and pans and things, since I've no time
    to be
A saint by doing lovely things in watching late with
    thee,
Or dreaming in the twilight, or storming heaven's
    gates.
Make me a saint by getting meals or washing up the
    plates.

Although I must have Martha's hands, I have a Mary
    mind;
And when I black the boots and shoes, thy sandals,
    Lord, I find.
I think of how they trod the earth each time I scrub
    the floor;
Accept this meditation, Lord. I haven't time for more.

Warm all the kitchen with thy love and warm it with
    thy peace.
Forgive me all my worrying, and make all grumbling
    cease.
Thou who didst love to give men food, in room or by
    the sea,
Accept this service that I do—I do it unto thee.
ELIZABETH TATE

The spirit of Love, wherever it is, is its own blessing
and happiness, because it is the truth and reality of
God in the soul; and therefore is in the same joy of
life, and is the same good to itself everywhere and on
every occasion. Would you know the blessing of all
blessings? It is this God of Love dwelling in your soul,
and killing every root of bitterness, which is the pain
and torment of every earthly, selfish love. For all wants
are satisfied, all disorders of nature are removed, no
life is any longer a burden, every day is a day of peace,
everything you meet becomes a help to you, because
everything you see or do is all done in the sweet,
gentle element of Love.
WILLIAM LAW

The King of love my shepherd is,
    Whose goodness faileth never:
I nothing lack if I am his,
    And he is mine for ever.

And so through all the length of days
    Thy goodness faileth never:
Good Shepherd, may I sing thy praise
    Within thy house for ever.
H. W. BAKER

With love our soul expands,
and is enlarged with the
greater life that attracts our
affections, and is purified
with its purity, and the soul
goes forth out of herself, to
live in the object of her love.
W. BERNARD ULLATHORNE

That same love, for which God
created and beautified the world,
is the only means for us to return
unto Him, who is the fountain
of our being.
ALGERNON SIDNEY

Let them seek God in all things,
putting off as far as possible
all love of creatures to place all
their love in the Creator, loving
Him in all creatures, and all
creatures in Him.
ST. IGNATIUS LOYOLA

Be ye therefore followers of God, as dear children;
And walk in love, as Christ also hath loved us, and
hath given himself for us an offering and a sacrifice to
God for a sweetsmelling savour.
EPHESIANS 5:1,2

Among so many, can He care?
Can special love be everywhere?
A myriad homes,—a myriad ways,—
And God's eye over every place?

I asked: my soul bethought of this;—
In just that very place of His
Where He hath put and keepeth you,
God hath no other thing to do!
A. D. T. WHITNEY

I know not where His islands lift
Their fronded palms in air;
I only know I cannot drift
Beyond His love and care.
JOHN GREENLEAF WHITTIER

The highest pinnacle of the spiritual life is not happy
joy in unbroken sunshine, but absolute and
undoubting trust in the love of God.
ANTHONY WILSON THOROLD

That Christ may dwell in your hearts by faith; that ye,
being rooted and grounded in love,
May be able to comprehend with all saints what is the
breadth, and length, and depth, and height;
And to know the love of Christ, which passeth
knowledge, that ye might be filled with all the fulness
of God.
Now unto him that is able to do exceeding abundantly
above all that we ask or think, according to the power
that worketh in us,
Unto him be glory in the church by Christ Jesus
throughout all ages, world without end. Amen.
EPHESIANS 3:17-21

O God, who comest with the dawn,
With light and love and cheer,
Grant me to know with burning heart
That Thou art always near.
Shine on the way in which I walk,
Upon the folk I meet;
And grant that friendliness and joy
May make each day complete.

CALVIN W. LAUFER

O love the Lord, all ye his saints: for the Lord
preserveth the faithful, and plentifully rewardeth the
proud doer.

PSALM 31:23

The perfect love of God
is a perfect union of wills
with God: that means the
inability to will anything
that God does not will.

THOMAS MERTON

More things are wrought by prayer
Than this world dreams of. Wherefore let thy voice
Rise like a fountain for me night and day.
For what are men better than sheep or goats
That nourish a blind life within the brain,
If, knowing God, they lift not hands in prayer
Both for themselves and those who call them friends?
For so the whole round earth is every way
Bound by gold chains about the feet of God.
ALFRED, LORD TENNYSON

We thank Thee, God, for eyes to see
    The beauty of the earth;
For ears to hear the words of love
    And happy sounds of mirth;
For minds that find new thoughts to think,
    New wonders to explore;
For health and freedom to enjoy
    The good Thou hast in store.
                          JEANETTE E. PERKINS

LORD OF ALL JOY

Lord of all hopefulness, Lord of all joy,
Whose trust, ever child-like, no cares could destroy,
Be there at our waking, and give us, we pray,
Your bliss in our hearts, Lord, at the break of the day.

Lord of all eagerness, Lord of all faith,
Whose strong hands were skilled
   at the plane and the lathe,
Be there at our labors, and give us, we pray,
Your strength in our hearts, Lord,
   at the noon of the day.

Lord of all kindliness, Lord of all grace,
Your hands swift to welcome, your arms to embrace,
Be there at our homing, and give us, we pray,
Your love in our hearts, Lord, at the eve of the day.

Lord of all gentleness, Lord of all calm,
Whose voice is contentment, whose presence is balm,
Be there at our sleeping, and give us, we pray,
Your peace in our hearts, Lord, at the end of the day.
JAN STRUTHER

GOD'S CHILDREN

We are all God's children and as such he views us—with love. Sydney Harris suggests that by looking at adults in this way we will see them in a more compassionate light.

See him as the child he was.

These seven simple one-syllable words have taken me half a lifetime to learn. But it has been worth the long hard-fought lesson.

For these are magic words: with them, you can rise above pettiness and spite, cruelty and arrogance and greed.

When you confront a man who shows these unattractive traits—see him as the child was.

Remember that he began his life with laughing expectancy, with trust, with warmth, desiring to give love and to take love.

And then remember that something happened to him—something he is not aware of—to turn the trust into suspicion, the warmth into wariness, the give-and-take into all-take and no-give.

See him as the child he was.

Behind the pomp or the rudeness, beneath the crust of meanness or coldness, begin to perceive the wistful little boy (or girl) who is hurt and disappointed and determined to strike back at the world.

Or the little boy who is frightened, and tightens his

jaw and clenches his fist to ward off some overwhelming fear that hovers deep in the dark past.

Or the little boy who was given too much too soon—and given *things* instead of *feelings*—and now can only clutch his power or his purse the way he used to clutch his teddy bear, because there is nothing else he feels is really his for keeps.

See him as the child he was.

Regard the faces as they pass you on the street: adult faces on the surface, but the child is lurking not too far beneath the skin—the child who eats too much because he craves the sweetness of affection, the child who drinks too much because he cannot face a motherless world, the child who brags and lies and cheats to wrest revenge for some huge indignity that is gnawing at his heart.

And then look again, closely, and you will see what the Book means when it calls all of us "God's children"—you will see a glimmer of hope behind the hate, a glint of humor behind the harshness, a touch of tenderness that no defensive wall can wholly obliterate.

Only in this way can we guard ourselves against responding in kind, against returning pettiness to the petty and cruelty to the cruel. And only in this way can we find the path to the green plateau of adulthood, where we can look down upon God's children with a sad but loving glance.

Do right, and God's recompense to you will be the power of doing more right. Give, and God's reward to you will be the spirit of giving more: a blessed spirit, for it is the Spirit of God himself, whose Life is the blessedness of giving. Love, and God will pay you with the capacity of more love; for love is Heaven—love is God within you.

F. W. ROBERTSON

"God is love" is not
one side of the truth,
but the whole truth
about God—there is no other side.

J. M. GIBBON

So to the calmly gathered thought
The innermost of life is taught,
The mystery dimly understood,
That love of God is love of good;
That to be saved is only this,—
Salvation from our selfishness.

JOHN GREENLEAF WHITTIER

I therefore, the prisoner of the Lord, beseech you that
ye walk worthy of the vocation wherewith ye are
called,
With all lowliness and meekness, with longsuffering,
forbearing one another in love;
Endeavouring to keep the unity of the Spirit in the
bond of peace.
EPHESIANS 4:1-3

Within Thy circling arms we lie,
O God! in Thy infinity:
Our souls in quiet shall abide,
Beset with love on every side.
ANONYMOUS

But the Lord is faithful, who shall stablish you, and
keep you from evil.
And we have confidence in the Lord touching you,
that ye both do and will do the things which we
command you.
And the Lord direct your hearts into the love of God,
and into the patient waiting for Christ.
II THESSALONIANS 3:3-5

And if some things I do not ask,
In my cup of blessing be,
I would have my spirit filled the more
With grateful love to Thee,—
More careful,—not to serve Thee much,
But to please Thee perfectly.

A. L. WARING

The Lord is my shepherd; I shall not want.
He maketh me to lie down in green pastures: he
leadeth me beside the still waters.
He restoreth my soul: he leadeth me in the paths of
righteousness for his name's sake.
Yea, though I walk through the valley of the shadow of
death, I will fear no evil: for thou art with me; thy rod
and thy staff they comfort me.
Thou preparest a table before me in the presence of
mine enemies: thou anointest my head with oil; my
cup runneth over.
Surely goodness and mercy shall follow me all the days
of my life: and I will dwell in the house of the Lord for
ever.

PSALM 23

Now thank we all our God,
With heart, and hands, and voices,
Who wondrous things hath done,
In whom his world rejoices;
Who from our mother's arms
Hath blessed us on our way
With countless gifts of love,
And still is ours to-day.

MARTIN RINKART

The highest example of justice, as Jesus saw, is not a
judge but a father, who knows his children separately
and considers what is right for each one of them, and
looks always to their good and happiness. God is
righteous because He is like a father.

E. F. SCOTT

He prayeth well who loveth well
    Both man and bird and beast;
He prayeth best who loveth best
    All things both great and small;
For the dear God who loveth us,
    He made and loveth all.

SAMUEL TAYLOR COLERIDGE

The Father who pities his children is the superlatively appropriate symbol of God, not because the worshiper, being one of the children, may hope to profit by paternal indulgence, but because all-reaching and infinitely patient love is the one thing supremely worshipful.

RALPH BARTON PERRY

I know not how that Bethlehem's babe
Could in the Godhead be;
I only know the manger child
Has brought God's life to me.

I know not how that Calvary's cross
A world from sin could free;
I only know its matchless love
Has brought God's love to me.

H. W. FARRINGTON

The sun does not look less upon one rose in the midst of a thousand millions of other flowers than if he looked down upon it alone. And God does not shed His love less upon one soul while He loves an infinity of others than if He loved it alone.

ST. FRANCIS OF SALES

Did we believe in him, I say not through faith, but
with a simple belief, yea . . . did we but believe and
know him, as we do another story, or as one of our
companions, we should then love him above all other
things, by reason of the infinite goodness, and
unspeakable beauty that is, and shines in him.
MICHEL DE MONTAIGNE

'Tis not enough that Christ was born
        Beneath the star that shone,
And earth was set that holy morn
        Within a golden zone.
He must be born within the heart
        Before he finds a throne,
And brings the day of love and good,
The reign of Christlike brotherhood.
                                    ANONYMOUS

There is nothing that makes us love a man so much as
praying for him. . . . By considering yourself as an
advocate with God for your neighbors and
acquaintances, you would never find it hard to be at
peace with them yourself.
WILLIAM LAW

What is Christian perfection?
The loving God with all our heart,
mind, soul, and strength. This
implies that no wrong temper,
none contrary to love, remains in
the soul; and that all the thoughts,
words, and actions are governed
by pure love.
JOHN WESLEY

And above all things have fervent charity among
yourselves: for charity shall cover the multitude of sins.
Use hospitality one to another without grudging.
As every man hath received the gift, even so minister
the same one to another, as good stewards of the
manifold grace of God.
I PETER 4:8-10

Love of friends, nuptial, heroical, profitable,
pleasant, honest, all these loves put together,
are little worth, if they proceed not from
a true Christian illuminated soul, if it
not be done for God's sake.
ROBERT BURTON

For I am persuaded, that neither death, nor life, nor
angels, nor principalities, nor powers, nor things
present, nor things to come,
Nor height, nor depth, nor any other creature, shall be
able to separate us from the love of God, which is in
Christ Jesus our Lord.
ROMANS 8:38,39

For now we see through a glass,
darkly; but then face to face:
now I know in part; but then
shall I know even as also I am
known.
And now abideth faith, hope,
and charity, these three; but
the greatest of these is charity.
I CORINTHIANS 13:12,13

He that loves God will soar aloft and take him wings;
and, leaving the earth, fly up to heaven, wander with
the sun and moon, stars, and that heavenly troop, God
Himself being his guide.
PHILO JUDAEUS

Then bless his holy Name,
Whose grace hath made thee whole,
Whose loving-kindness crowns thy days!
O bless the Lord, my soul!
JAMES MONTGOMERY

Love, being the highest Godly principle, is the virtue
of all virtues, from whence they flow forth. Love, being
the greatest majesty, is the power of all powers, from
whence they severally operate.
JAKOB BOEHME

Lord of all being, throned afar,
Thy glory flames from sun and star;
Center and soul of every sphere,
Yet to each loving heart how near!
OLIVER WENDELL HOLMES

What is love? It is the sweetness of life; it is the sweet,
tender, melting nature of God, flowing up through his
seed of life into the creature, and of all things making
the creature most like unto himself, both in nature
and operation.
ISAAC PENINGTON

God is to me that creative Force,
behind and in the universe, who
manifests Himself as energy, as life,
as order, as beauty, as thought,
as conscience, as love, and who is
self-revealed supremely in the creative
Person of Jesus of Nazareth.
HENRY SLOANE COFFIN

We talk about God's remembering us, as if it were a
special effort. But if we could only know how truly we
belong to God, it would be different. God's
remembrance of us is the natural claiming of our life
by Him as true part of His own.
PHILLIPS BROOKS

Wherefore I put thee in remembrance
that thou stir up the gift of God, which
is in thee by the putting on of my hands.
For God hath not given us the spirit of
fear; but of power, and of love . . .
II TIMOTHY 1:6,7

This is my commandment,
That ye love one another,
as I have loved you.
Greater love hath no man
than this, that a man lay
down his life for his friends.

JOHN 15:12,13

If divine love is the author of all existence, it follows
that nothing can exist wherein love cannot find
expression.

A. C. TURNER

True prayer, and that which is best,
lies in whatever unites us to God,
whatever enables us to enjoy Him, to
appreciate Him, to rejoice in His Glory,
and to love Him as one's very own.

JACQUES BÉNIGNE BOSSUET

And above all these things put on charity,
which is the bond of perfectness.
And let the peace of God rule in your hearts
. . . . and be ye thankful.
COLOSSIANS 3:14,15

Love is the greatest thing that God can give us; for
Himself is love; and it is the greatest thing we can give
to God.
JEREMY TAYLOR

Our prayer and God's mercy are like two buckets in a
well; while one ascends, the other descends.
ARTHUR HOPKINS

. . . whither thou goest, I will go;
and where thou lodgest, I will lodge:
thy people shall be my people,
and thy God my God.
RUTH 1:16

Whosoever believeth that Jesus
is the Christ is born of God:
and every one that loveth him
that begat loveth him also
that is begotten of him.
By this we know that we love
the children of God,
when we love God, and keep
his commandments.

I JOHN 5:1,2

All that is good, all that is true,
all that is beautiful, all that is
beneficent be it great or small,
be it perfect or fragmentary,
natural as well as supernatural,
moral as well as material,
comes from God.

JOHN HENRY NEWMAN

Love is our highest word, and the synonym of God.
RALPH WALDO EMERSON

WORDS OF INNOCENCE—WORDS OF TRUTH

The idea of "God is Love" has been expressed in writing through the ages. Perhaps it is best defined in these responses received by writer Ruth Harley when she asked a group of children, "What does God mean to you?"

God is your feelings. He is someone to turn to when you're down. He's hope. God is love. He makes you happy when you're scared.

TARA, age 12

God is what is inside you. He is what makes you think and what makes you love.

DOUG, age 12

God is love. God is life. God made the stars. He made plants and water. God made people. God made fish and bugs. God loves us. God makes trees.

EDEN, age 8

God to me is flowers in bloom and people loving people. God means peace. God means all good things and LIFE.

LAURIE, age 9

God is love. He made the world. He takes the ones that are died. He is life like in trees. He makes nature, He makes me and others. God makes the sun, God makes everything.

THOMAS, age 8

God may be just a name for nothing. When we pray, we say "God" because we need a name for the feeling that we get. I also think God is another name for love, kindness, truth, peace, joy, and so forth.

CHRIS, age 12

God is a thought of goodness to help others to do good things. He made the world and nature.

ELISE, age 8

God is peace!!!! Love Joy Peace
TAMMIE, age 9

I'm very glad that there is a God. If there wasn't, we wouldn't be here. All we might be would be clumps of grass.
DAVID, age 7

God is a name for all good things.
KATHY, age 12

God means love to me. He also gives me something that makes me feel He's my father. I also remember a lot of stories about Him. I remember God as one great man.
BRENDA, age 8

God is a name for everything in the world. God is Love and it's Joy and Friendship.
SARAH, age 12

Acknowledgments

The editor and the publisher have made every effort to trace the ownership of all copyrighted material and to secure permission from copyright holders of such material. In the event of any question arising as to the use of any material the publisher and editor, while expressing regret for inadvertent error, will be pleased to make the necessary corrections in future printings. Thanks are due to the following authors, publishers, publications and agents for permission to use the material indicated.

HOUGHTON MIFFLIN COMPANY, for excerpt from *Majority of One* by Sydney J. Harris, copyright © 1957 by Sydney J. Harris.

THE HYMN SOCIETY OF AMERICA, for "I know not how that Bethlehem's Babe" by Harry Webb Farrington, copyright 1930 by The Hymn Society of America.

OXFORD UNIVERSITY PRESS, for "Lord of all hopefulness, Lord of all joy" by Jan Struther, from *Enlarged Songs of Praise.*

UNITED CHURCH PRESS, for "We thank Thee, God, for eyes to see" by Jeannette E. Perkins, copyright 1936, 1964 by The Pilgrim Press.

Photo Credits

Klauss Brahmst—Cover, p. 15; Penny Pederson—p. 2; State Development Office of Maine—p. 6, p. 38; Four By Five, Inc.—p. 11, p. 30; Eric Sanford—p. 19; Jay Johnson—p. 23; Gene Ruestmann—p. 35; Stanford Burns—p. 42; State of Vermont—p. 47; Wyoming Travel Commission—p. 51; Bruce Ando—p. 55.

Selected by Priscilla Shepard
Set in Palatino,
a type face designed
by Herman Zapf.
Designed by Thomas James Aaron